KID'S STORIES

A COLLECTION OF GREAT MINECRAFT SHORT STORIES FOR CHILDREN

UNOFFICIAL MINECRAFT FICTION

BlockBoy

Table of Contents

The Bold Thief

Who's stealing?

RolyPoly wondered if he was dreaming. All the diamonds in his treasure chest were gone! And this was the third time it was happening. RolyPoly scratched his head. He thought it must be one of the players. He had heard of players stealing grains and other things.

*"RolyPoly wondered if he was dreaming. All the
diamonds in his treasure chest were gone!"*

"But why is he stealing again and again from
me?" RolyPoly thought. He was worried.

RolyPoly looked at the hills in the distance.
He chose a quiet spot in the Minecraft
Universe, as far away from others as he could
manage. He did not want to see any players,
villagers or mobs.

He decided to look around to see if he could
find anyone. The forest was very close by,
and RolyPoly gripped his sword tight as he
walked and looked around. He turned back
to look at his fortress proudly.

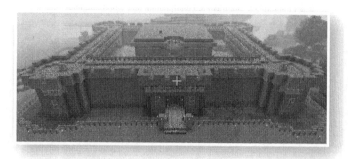

"He turned back to look at his fortress proudly."

Tough luck

He had spent so many hours placing block after block, building it with great care. RolyPoly wanted it to be the best fortress in the world. Or at least he hoped it would be.

He'd spent a whole day digging a moat around the entire fortress and filling it up with water. He knew that Endermen sometimes stole blocks and the water would keep them away.

Yet, here was a thief who had crossed the moat, climbed the high wall, broke the treasure chest and escaped away with all the diamonds. RolyPoly had gone out just for a while to look for food, and the thief had taken the diamonds in those few minutes.

Last time it had been his diamond sword and even before that, two emeralds and some gold ingots.

A Trap

RolyPoly was very angry.

"I'll catch the thief," he kept muttering to himself. He had to catch the thief and put an end to this.

He wanted a trap, a simple one that would work.

RolyPoly chose a nice spot along a long corridor and started digging in the corner. He dug deeper and deeper until it was several blocks deep. He placed a ladder, leapt out of the hole and looked down. He was very happy. It was a deep, deep hole. He placed a block of wool on top and wrote a sign that read: 'Diamonds Below'.

He hoped the thief would come this time. RolyPoly rubbed his hands in delight. He decided to go out again. The thief would then come inside the fortress and find the sign.

RolyPoly wandered around for a bit. Then he came back to his fortress after an hour.

Outsmarted

"I wonder if the thief came and went..." said RolyPoly loudly.

He went up the stairs and rushed along the corridor. He was dismayed to see that the wool block was intact. The sign was also there.

Wait.

The sign looked different. It did not read 'Diamonds Below'. Instead, it read 'Silly Traps are only for fools!'

He hurried over to the other treasure chest in the room nearby. The emeralds he'd kept there in the morning had gone!

RolyPoly felt like crying. This was no ordinary thief.

That night he decided to hide and watch out for the thief. He went out and brought back a diamond that he had mined. He hoped that the thief noticed it, whoever he was.

Face-to-Face with the Thief

He went into the fortress, placed it in a treasure chest and hid right behind it.

Late in the night, when RolyPoly had almost fallen asleep, he heard the sound of footsteps.

"The thief," RolyPoly whispered to himself and waited.

When the thief opened the treasure chest, RolyPoly sprang out from his hiding place. He had a sword in his hand.

But when he saw who it was, RolyPoly was taken aback. It was not a player.

It was the one and only Herobrine!

"It was the one and only Herobrine!"

"I didn't believe you existed!" RolyPoly said. His hands shook as he tried to hold his sword steadily.

Fighting Herobrine is Tough

"Of course," said Herobrine, laughing wickedly. His eyes glowed. It made RolyPoly feel more uneasy.

"His eyes glowed. It made RolyPoly feel more uneasy."

"Prepare to perish," RolyPoly cried, lifting his sword high up in the air.

But Herobrine was too quick for him.

CLING! CLANG! CRASH!

Herobrine and RolyPoly fought with their swords.

RolyPoly realized that Herobrine was very powerful. He was so good at sword fighting! Every strike was powerful and RolyPoly knew that he had to do something fast. If he ran out, there was every chance that Herobrine would take the fortress for his own.

"He was so good at sword fighting!"

Out in the Open

The only other way was to lead him downstairs slowly and out of the fortress where they could fight out in the open. Slowly RolyPoly stepped down the stairs, fighting Herobrine all the time. They fought in the great hall and Herobrine was becoming more powerful.

By a great stroke of luck, RolyPoly swung his sword sideways and just as Herobrine ducked, he slipped and fell on the ground. RolyPoly opened the door quickly and stepped outside. Herobrine followed him.

They fought out in the open. RolyPoly was very tired but he got lucky a second time!

The Lucky Break

A skeleton armed with a bow and arrow had appeared behind Herobrine. Just as Herobrine turned around, he was face to face with it. Herobrine moved away quickly. His sword fell on the ground and Herobrine pulled out his bow and an arrow. He ran to hide behind a bush, forgetting all about RolyPoly. RolyPoly grabbed Herobrine's sword and went inside his fortress.

"A skeleton armed with a bow and arrow had appeared behind Herobrine."

He pulled the drawbridge over and shut the big wooden door. RolyPoly felt safe, at least for a few minutes. He knew that Herobrine would come back to get his sword.

He had to think of a way to send Herobrine away; otherwise he might have to forget his precious fortress. He knew that he didn't want to fight with Herobrine again.

Then RolyPoly remembered something. There was a way to get rid of Herobrine!

The 'Don't Come Back' Portal

He went to the basement, opened the door and took some obsidian blocks from his inventory. With the blocks, he made a frame for a nether portal. When it was ready, he took some steel and flint and lit it up. Now here was the interesting part - RolyPoly entered through the portal and placed a TNT block close to the entrance, enough to hit but not kill anybody.

"When it was ready, he took some steel and flint and lit it up."

Just before teleporting back to his fortress, RolyPoly hit it hard and rushed through the portal. He was back in his fortress. RolyPoly was so excited! His job was done. All he had to do now was to make Herobrine enter through the door in the basement. He prayed that Herobrine shouldn't have flint and steel with him to reignite the portal.

RolyPoly hid outside the door, behind a pillar. He knew that Herobrine would come in search of his sword.

RolyPoly waited. His heart was beating rapidly. Then he hears slow footsteps. Someone was coming down the stairs. The eyes glowed and RolyPoly shivered. It was Herobrine, no doubt! Quickly, he took a tiny pebble in his pocket and threw it near the door.

Trapped in the Nether!

Herobrine looked in the direction of the noise and ran inside. He saw the portal right in front of him. He tried to stop but it was too late! Herobrine went through the portal and landed in the Nether world on the other side. Herobrine fell on the ground and the TNT exploded.

BOOM!

...The portal was destroyed! Herobrine couldn't return to RolyPoly's fortress.

Herobrine realized that he had been fooled! He felt very angry. He knew that he didn't have any flint and steel with him. Until he found a way back, he was trapped in the Nether. And also without his sword! Herobrine wondered how he was going to face the mobs in the Nether. When he saw a magma cube in the distance, he ran away quickly to hide.

Mission: Success

RolyPoly waited anxiously on the other side. Every second he was afraid that Herobrine would find his way back, but when he did not return for a long, long time, he heaved a big sigh of relief.

He'd got rid of the thief! But there were other things to do. But first, he hung Herobrine's sword on the wall, as a mark of his victory. RolyPoly wanted to make his fortress really safe so that no one could enter. He didn't want any more thieves stealing his things. He also wanted to learn to make better traps!

"But first, he hung Herobrine's sword on the wall, as a mark of his victory."

Life goes on in Minecraft World

RolyPoly left his fortress and went to a diamond mine not far from there. He had his bow ready. When he saw a zombie in the distance, he aimed his bow straight at it.

ZWANG! WHIZZZ!

Two arrows flew by, and the zombie fell to the ground. RolyPoly went into the mine and got two diamonds. He was glad that he didn't have to worry about them getting stolen anymore!

There was always the risk of finding spiders in the mine, but RolyPoly was feeling very good indeed! He had defeated Herobrine and he was in a great mood. He knew that he could deal with any mob, with just a little effort!

Taming the Bully

Meet the Bully

Jacob was a big bully. He was a terror for the little kids. They ran away when they saw him around!

He did mean things. Jacob pushed kids from swings. He leapt out of bushes and knocked his friends on the ground. He put spiders on his classmates' desk and stuck gum under the teacher's desk.

He played terrible pranks too! He spilled ink on books. Sometimes he placed a bucket of water above the door to drench the first unlucky person to enter the classroom.

The kids wanted to teach him a lesson! Especially Rory and Fred who sat just behind Jacob in class, and knew all his terrible pranks.

Big Plans

"Yesterday, Jacob pushed a kid from the swing..." Fred said.

"Too bad... we need to stop him." Rory remarked.

"What should we do?" Fred asked.

"We'll invite him to play Minecraft with us and show him our pranks," Rory smiled.

"Great idea! We have a few tricks that'll be perfect for Jacob," said Fred. "We'll teach him a good lesson!"

The Invitation

During recess, Rick suddenly turned around.

"Hey, Jacob, do you play Minecraft?" he asked.

"Yup," said Jacob, biting into his sandwich.

"Want to join us tonight? We're planning something big," Fred said.

"Sure!" Jacob nodded.

Jacob was excited. Later at home, he settled down comfortably and switched on his gaming console. He had been playing Minecraft for a while and knew quite a few things. He was so happy when Fred and Rick invited him to join them. Jacob made plans to steal their stuff or play tricks on them!

Enter: Minecraft

Jacob was in a great mood. The Minecraft world was exciting and fun. Here, a player could do so many different things. What he loved most was the tricks and pranks of course! He'd played pranks on his friends in Minecraft too! He thought of Rory and Fred as his new victims.

Jacob saw Rory and Fred in the distance and waved. They were walking towards him. He pointed to his fortress. Jacob was proud of it. He'd built it with great care and it had taken him a really long time.

"He pointed to his fortress. Jacob was proud of it. He'd built it with great care and it had taken him a really long time."

Jacob was wondering if he should take them to the basement where he had many traps laid out.

"Come along inside," Jacob said. He noticed that only Rory was there.

"Where's Fred?" he asked.

"I think he went that way... He should be here soon," said Rory.

Almost immediately, Fred came running towards them.

"Where were you?" asked Jacob.

"What happened? You look scared..." said Rory.

"Had to fight off two Endermen..." Fred said breathlessly.

Suddenly, there were loud noises.

CLUCK! CLUCK!

PECK! PECK!!!

BAAA! BAAAAAA!!!

It looked as if an entire farm of animals were agitated.

Farm Scenes

"Is that noise coming from your farm?" Fred asked in surprise.

"Wow, you must have a big bunch of chickens there!"

Jacob looked puzzled.

"What? I don't have any chickens..." he said and went to check his farm.

He stopped and stared in surprise.

It was the weirdest sight ever!

There were hundreds of chickens roaming around, clucking noisily and pecking at the ground and each other.

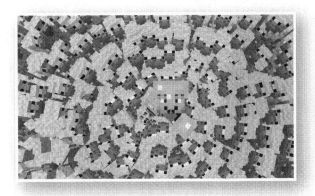

"There were hundreds of chickens roaming around"

All his sheep were out of the barn, roaming about outside. Worse still, they were in different shades of pink and yellow.

Shades of Doubt

Jacob didn't know what to say or do. He was shocked. Nothing like this had ever happened to him before. He looked at Rory and Fred, but they looked so innocent and surprised. Jacob was sure that they were not responsible for the mess. He wondered who was doing this to him.

Jacob shrugged. "I'm sure it's some stupid player out here somewhere. I'll deal with him later," said Jacob. "Come inside!"

Rory held Jacob's arm.

"Are you sure it's a player? What if it's something else?" he said.

Jacob looked at him strangely. "What do you mean? Mobs don't do that..."

"Well, it could be..." said Fred quietly. "You never know!"

Jacob felt a shiver run down his spine.

"This place seems unsafe. Come let's go over to where we're building a fortress. You can help us!" Rory said.

Jacob didn't want to help, but he still wanted to play some pranks on them, so he went with them.

Exploding Tree

Fred got to work quickly.

While Rory was talking to Jacob, Fred chose a nice big tree and climbed it. He placed a redstone torch on the top part of the trunk. Then he placed a block over the torch and placed a second redstone torch over it. Then he positioned a TNT block close to the second torch and climbed down.

He grinned and flashed a *thumbs up* when Rory looked at him.

Then Rory spoke to Jacob, "Hey do you think you'll be able to chop down that tree? We'll use it to make some planks!"

Jacob was thinking of a great prank to play on them. He was still thinking about it as he took his axe and chopped the tree. In the meantime, the block holding the second torch shifted, and the redstone torch fell straight on the TNT block...

BOOM!

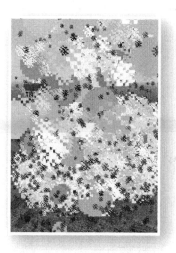

"BOOM!"

Jacob's axe flew out of his hands and he fell backwards with such force that his neck hurt. Fred and Rory came running over.

"You alright? What happened to that tree?" Rory asked.

"I don't know," Jacob wailed, rubbing his neck. His cheeks were streaked with black soot and he looked a sorry sight.

"I think it's the work of something evil..." Fred said.

Jacob looked at him in surprise.

"What do you mean?" he asked.

"Come over there... we'll explain," said Rory

The Mysterious Creature

Rory and Fred took him inside the small structure they'd built.

"Did you know that a new mob has been added in Minecraft?" Fred asked casually.

Jacob's eyes opened wide. Then he laughed.

"You think I'm a fool to believe your story?" Jacob asked.

"Uh, didn't you get any mail about that?" Rory asked, looking surprised. "Everybody has got it!"

Jacob looked at them, hoping that they'd laugh, but they looked very serious.

"Stop joking..." said Jacob, but he didn't sound so sure anymore.

"So... what kind of creature is it?"

Knock at the door

"We'll have to find out, but I think it could be really dangerous," said Fred.

"Rory is going over to see if the creature is anywhere around... and also bring back some food," Fred said.

Rory nodded and went out, slamming the door.

Hardly minutes after he'd left, Fred and Jacob heard a knock.

KNOCK! SLAM! BAM!

"Who's that?" said Fred. Jacob looked up, surprised.

"Rory doesn't knock that way and it's not any of the usual mobs either," Fred remarked.

"Then what is it?" Jacob asked.

"I think it's the creature... we'll have to destroy it!" Fred whispered.

Knocking Continues

Jacob watched anxiously as Fred crept slowly towards the window.

TAP! TAP! TAP!

The tapping continued and Rory had still not returned.

Jacob was really scared. He'd never heard or seen anything like this before. Fred peered out of the window and then turned around.

"Jacob was really scared."

"What?" Jacob asked in a whisper.

"Go outside slowly..." Fred whispered. "The creature is out there..."

"Can't you go and strike it?" Jacob asked.

"You have a diamond sword... it's better than mine. Go!" said Fred.

The Great Fall

Jacob held his sword high and crept out of the door.

He was so busy dreaming of being called a hero by Fred and Rory for killing the mysterious creature, that he did not see the gaping hole just outside the door.

SPLAT! SPLOOSH!

He slipped and went straight into the hole. It was full of water and except for a bruise, he was not hurt. But Jacob was furious. He heard loud laughter and realized that Fred and Rory had played a mean trick on him. Since the pit was a little deep, he had no way of coming out and had to wait for one of them to pull him out.

Eventually, they helped him out of the pit. Jacob sat down on the ground, just outside the pit. He was soaking wet and shivering.

Everyone Hates Mean Pranks

"I hate it! I hate you guys," Jacob hissed. "You made up everything. About the mysterious mob and you played all those terrible pranks!"

"But we thought you love pranks?" Rory asked.

"No, I hate it," said Jacob.

"And everyone hates it too when you play mean tricks on them," said Fred.

"Yeah, you have to stop doing that," added Rory.

"Thanks for your great advice," said Jacob and walked off in a huff.

Bully Learns His Lesson

That night, Jacob lay on his bed and thought about it. He hated Rory and Fred. But he remembered what they told him. At least, they'd played tricks on him only in a virtual world, and that hurt so much. Jacob played real pranks on people that actually hurt.

Then he slowly realized his mistake.

"Maybe I should change," he said to himself.

Jacob did change! He didn't play pranks that often and he stopped bullying the kids.

Rory and Fred believe that Minecraft helped change the ways of a bully. They still played with Jacob once in a while, but no more pranks or tricks! They had plenty of fun, exploring and trying out new things!

Lost Love

The Dark City

Alex is a young and brave little boy but he is very sad. He has come back from his hostel to his hometown during his school vacation only to see that all his friends and neighbors have started to hate each other. Nobody cares for each other anymore. They argue over petty matters. They are all gloomy and depressed. Now Alex doesn't have any friends. He is not willing to talk to anyone for the fear of being scolded by an elder. He is not willing to play with anyone for the fear of being pushed or bullied by the youngsters. Alex is highly concerned about the state of his city.

The Blue Bird

One fine evening, Alex was looking at the lush green lawn from his bedroom's window wanting very desperately to go out and play with his friends. Suddenly, he saw a big blue bird coming towards him. It came and settled down near him. Alex was surprised to see it and noticed a piece of paper and a map in its beak.

"Suddenly, he saw a big blue bird coming towards him."

"What's that? And who are you?" Alex cried out.

The bird stayed quiet. Alex moved forward and with trembling hands, took the paper and read it out aloud.

The note said, "The love essence has been extracted from people's hearts by an evil witch. You must look for this love essence in the Fiery Dragon's room inside the Nether Fortress."

The map showed the direction to the fortress.

Alex Sets Out For An Adventure

Immediately Alex decided to leave for the Nether Fortress. His parents will not know, they will think he has gone to sleep, he thought. He could hear his siblings. They were busy arguing over some silly matter in the room next door. He quickly packed up a bag for himself and set off on the blue bird's back.

The blue bird was living with an old lady who had got to know the secret of the evil witch. She along with her pet bird had flown in the same way to the fortress in an attempt to obtain the love potion, but she had been kidnapped by the evil witch. Now the old lady was a prisoner in a secret chamber in the Fiery Dragon's room. She had successfully managed to somehow write a note and send the bird for help.

Luckily for Alex, the bird knew its way around and flew in the desired direction to take Alex to his destination as fast as she could. It was now night time and darkness prevailed over the city. Alex wanted the journey to be over but it took quite some time.

It was morning by the time they reached a vast open ground. The sun had risen and Alex could feel his stomach rumbling. He walked now with the blue bird walking behind him. They found an apple tree and they ate as much as they wanted. Now the blue bird bid farewell and flew away to its nest, leaving Alex alone in his journey to the Nether fortress. Then Alex filled up a bucket of water for himself wondering it may be used to quench his thirst afterwards. Then he started walking in the direction of the fortress as it was told in the map. He hoped to find some weapons or tools that would be helpful for him.

Encounter with An Old Man

All of a sudden an old man came towards him. He said: "where are you going, young one?"

"All of a sudden an old man came towards him."

Alex answered, "I am going to the Nether fortress to look for the love potion in the Fiery Dragon's room."

The old man said, "There is danger in the fortress, and the Fiery Dragon is a very dangerous creature. You must not go there."

But Alex said, "I must go there. I want the love potion. I want my people to love and care for each other. I must go for the sake of my people."

The old man replied, "Don't tell me that I didn't warn you, little master. And if you must go there, take this ring with you. This is no ordinary ring. It has magical powers and will allow you to be invisible for one whole minute when you fix it in your middle finger."

He handed Alex a shiny silver ring that he carefully kept in his pocket.

The Nether Fortress

The old man disappeared from sight and Alex continued walking across the open stretched ground. There were huge mountains that could be seen now and according to the map he was following, there was a path in one of the caves that led to the fortress. He reached the mountain bearing. Suddenly, one of the volcanoes erupted!

"Suddenly, one of the volcanoes erupted!"

"Oh God, What should I do now?" he thought.

He did not have much time because huge amounts of hot lava started flowing along the sides of the mountain at once. He rushed into the cave and took shelter. The cave had a wide rocky path leading straightway out from some distance. He could see light at its exit and knew that he was not far from the opening at the other end.

He started walking towards the far end when he noticed a group of strange looking creatures coming towards him. When they came near, he saw that they were Zombie Pigmen of all sizes. Some were old and stout while others were tall and slim. They ran from Alex's side and did not dare to hurt or even come near him. One little Zombie even dropped his golden sword that Alex picked up after they had gone.

Now Alex ran to the exit of the cave and saw another stretch of vast ground in front of him. Far across he could now see the mysterious Nether fortress. He walked behind the trees so the watchmen at the gate would not notice him. He reached the gate and quickly wore the magical ring that the old man gave him. He now became invisible and rushed towards the entrance. In one minute's time, he had hid himself behind a huge fireplace inside the well-lit lobby of the fortress.

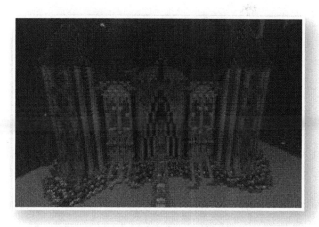

"Far across he could now see the mysterious Nether fortress"

"Yes! I have successfully reached the inside of the fortress", he said to himself.

Several Endermen were keeping guard outside the different rooms in the castle but Alex did not get frightened at all. That was a piece of cake for him. He took out his bucket of water and splashed water over them. One by one, the Endermen all fled and Alex was free to go to the Fiery Dragon's room.

The Fiery Dragon

He opened the door and saw a huge bright room that had enormous chandeliers and magnificent Chinese carvings on the walls. The poor old lady was tied to a chair on one side of the room. An enormous dragon was breathing fire and was waiting to attack him. Alex took out his golden sword but it seemed too small. His sword did not a weapon that he could use to defeat the mighty dragon. He did not know what to do.

*"An enormous dragon was breathing fire
and was waiting to pounce upon him."*

Suddenly the blue bird flew in from the window. She was carrying a strange looking bottle. She threw the bottle towards Alex. He opened it immediately. At once a strong odor of coffee and lemon was released from it. This strange potion put the Fiery Dragon to sleep. Alex heaved a sigh of relief! He could not believe his eyes when he saw that the dragon which he was so terribly afraid of, was lying asleep near his feet.

He ran to the old lady and untied her. With her help, he lifted up the mantel piece slab to find a little bottle containing the love essence. The old lady and Alex took the little bottle and climbed on the blue bird's back again. They flew until they reached their city. They both now sprinkled the love essence on all the people around them. Instantly, the people started coming back to their normal selves. Those who were being rude were now saying sorry for their behavior. Those who were not listening to their elders promised not to do that again. Those who did not want to take care of others realized how wrong they were and promised to be helpful and caring for each other.

Life Goes On....

Meanwhile, the blue bird flew away to her native forest in the south. The old lady had nowhere to go and Alex insisted on making her stay at his home. His parents happily allowed her to stay with them. Now the old lady lives with Alex and together they often talk about the great adventure they had!

Tessa's Strange Encounter

"HA HA HA HA HA," roared the nasty Witch, while stirring a big pot of her brew, "I will make you my prisoner! I will not let you go, you thin creature."

Steffy Is Lost

Tessa was a thin little 8 year old girl. She had gone camping to a forest with her parents. Tessa was enjoying the company of a few of her friends. She was very fond of her pet dog, Steffy. In the afternoon during tea while everyone was having a nap, she found Steffy missing.

She wandered off alone to search for him.

"Steffy, Steffy, where are youuuu?" she shouted. But Steffy did not respond. In this search she did not realize that she had gone deep into the big, dark forest and that she was now very far from the camping site.

Tessa got tired after some time and sat on a rock, worried about her poor little dog.

"What has happened to him? Has he hurt his legs? Maybe his leg has got stuck in a thorny bush?" she wondered.

Tessa Is Caught Too!

Suddenly somebody dashed towards her from the back and caught hold of her.

It was the evil Witch! She had come out into the forest to look for some special ingredients that she could add to her pot of broth.

"It was the evil Witch!"

A while later Tessa found herself inside the Witch's house. Tessa was sitting and trembling alongside Steffy who had also been captured by the Witch. Luckily the Witch had decided not to add any humans in her brew. When Tessa found out, she heaved a sigh of relief. But she was worried about Steffy.

"Oh please, oh please, Witch, Steffy is very dear to me", she shouted and started weeping bitterly.

"Only if you go into the dungeon and bring me three very, very slimy and spooky creatures, only then will I spare Steffy. Otherwise, your dog must go," said the Witch and again roared into laughter.

Tessa was frightened but for Steffy's sake she agreed to go into the dungeon. Steffy was put into the cage. Tessa had only one hour to bring the creatures to the Witch. "If an hour goes by, and you are still not back, then I will put your dog in my brew," warned the Witch. With this warning, she threw poor Tessa into the dark dungeon.

The Dungeon

Tessa got up and with great courage started to explore the dungeon. She noticed that the dungeon is actually a maze. This made had many paths leading to mysterious places. She walked for a time until she stumbled upon a door. She opened the door and went inside the dimly lit room only to see that it was empty. She started to walk towards the exit when suddenly a Wither skeleton popped out. The skeleton was dark and scary and she got frightened. She took out a stick from her pocket to scare the skeleton away but it still continued to move forward. Tessa screamed loudly and turned around. She ran back outside from the same door she had entered.

A Friendly Ghast

Now she saw a jelly like creature coming towards her. She realized that it was a Ghast. She could not believe it and thought the Ghast would shoot a fireball at her. She started crying. The Ghast was terrified. He did not like seeing little children crying.

"She realized that it was a Ghast."

"Poor thing, why are you crying?" asked the soft hearted Ghast.

Tessa was amazed to see a talking monster. She told the whole story to the Ghast. The Ghast listened to her story patiently and promised to come with her to save her and her dog from the evil Witch.

"I will crack and I will screech and I will let the whole Witch's brew explode," he said.

A Hungry Spider

Tessa was relieved. Now she started searching for the next creature. The Ghast was very helpful and guided Tessa to a spider's web. The spider had gone to the orchid to pick up some grapes but sadly it came back with none. Tessa had been carrying a bunch of grapes in her bag and she took them out and offered some to the spider. The Spider was very happy to see them. He promised Tessa to be part of their journey if she continued to feed him a grape every 10 minutes. Tessa saw that the bunch of grapes she was holding and she knew that they would be more than enough for the whole journey. She agreed to feed the spider the grapes and continued with her search for the last creature. And so she walked with the Ghast and Spider.

A Strange Fish

They turned left, then right, the right again. They weren't sure where to go. They saw a light at the end of a path and walked there. When they came near the light, they saw that a huge pool of water had been formed into a crater in the earth. Various fish and sea animals were occupying it. On the edge of the pool, she noticed a strange looking purple fish with green dots over its body and two horn like tentacles sticking out of its head.

"This is a very, very slimy and spooky creature," she thought.

She picked up a bucket lying nearby and filled it up with water. With the help of the Spider and the Ghast, she managed to lift up the fish and put it in the bucket.

Now Tessa had three creatures with her. She had remembered to throw grapes to the Spider who had now become her friend. On the way back, the Ghast explained the Spider and the Fish the whole story. They both promised Tessa to remain faithful to her. They also assured her that they were not afraid of the Witch. The Fish was especially very happy to hear this.

She said, very excitedly, "Oh, that nasty Witch is responsible for me looking like this. She cast a magic spell over my body and changed my color and shape. Now is the time to seek revenge."

Together, the three creatures roared, "We will defeat the evil Witch!"

Back to The Witch's House

Tessa had now was back to the place in the dungeon where she had been thrown in. She called out to the Witch.

"I have brought three very, very slimy and spooky creatures just like you asked me."

The Witch looked from the window of her kitchen down into the dungeon and saw Tessa standing there with the spider, Ghast and the fish. She was pleased to see them and she quickly opened the door to Tessa.

"Come in, come in, my dear," she said. Tessa stepped into the kitchen. She did not like the rotten and unpleasant smell of the brew that was being cooked. She immediately stepped away from it.

"Here, you are", the Witch said, opening the cage, "you can take your dog and stay in the other room. Don't try to escape because I have cast a magic spell over my doors that will turn children like you into slimy creatures. So stay away from them unless you want to become a slimy creature."

The Witch took the spider into her hand. It started crawling up her hands until it reached her shoulders. The Ghast sat on her hands, while the fish jumped up to reach her head. They all started to hiss and shout. The Witch started laughing wickedly. One by one she snatched the poor creatures and threw them in her boiling brew. The creatures were strong and resistant to heat. They shook and cracked and a big explosion occurred in the pot.

HISSSSSSS.....CRAAAAACK...... SCREEEEEEEECH

BANG! BANG! THUMP! THUMP!

With a loud bang, the pot broke and the brew spread all over the walls of the room. The Witch was standing close by and she got burnt with the hot brew. She fell down on the kitchen floor with a big thud. She lay on the floor unconscious.

The three creatures had done it! They had cracked and they had screeched and they had let the whole Witch's brew explode! They now returned safely to their habitat, down into the dungeon. The fish had also returned back to its original appearance. The magic was not working anymore.

Tessa Escapes

Meanwhile, as soon as the explosion had occurred, Tessa with Steffy in her hands had managed to escape out of a broken window that was lying open. She climbed out and ran as fast as she could and did not even dare to look behind. Into the forest she ran. She ran over the hills and was relieved to see her parents. Tessa ran to them and they embraced her with a lot of joy. She told them the whole story and promised them never to go anywhere alone without their permission.

Skeleton War

The Diamond Mine

In the Overworld, just beyond a forest there was an enormous diamond mine. It was thought to be one of the biggest mines in Minecraft. Players came from different places, armed with their pickaxes and other tools, in search of the diamonds. The villagers came too, because they knew that they could exchange the diamonds for other useful things with the players.

"In the Overworld, just beyond a forest there was an enormous diamond mine."

But the problem was that it was not easy to even step in through the entrance, let alone mine the diamonds there. Players came alone or in groups and tried to find a way into the mine, but it was of no use.

That was too bad, wasn't it? The diamonds were out there ready for grabs, yet nobody could get it...

Are you wondering what was possibly wrong and why it was not possible to go inside?

Skeletons Guarding the Treasure

You see, the mine was guarded fiercely by a group of skeletons armed with swords and bows. Nobody knew where they came from or why they were guarding the mine. But they remained there and fought anyone who dared to come close to the mine.

If ever any player ventured within the 16 block radius, the skeletons chased him in a group, some with swords and others with bows. The arrows whizzed by everywhere! The players who did manage to escape from their clutches, never returned to the mine.

The players tried different ways to enter the mine. Some tried to tunnel into the mine, but they were caught by skeletons that guarded the place so carefully. Others tried different ways to fight the skeletons, only to be shot or driven away.

The Big Failure

MinerJack was one of the players who were particularly interested in defeating the skeletons. He came with his friends on a mission to defeat the skeletons.

The first time they went, they had no plans. They were all armed with swords and enchanted bows and arrows.

"We'll take the skeletons by surprise," said MinerJack. He pointed a way that was far away from the entrance but gave them good hiding places. Things would have gone fine if a player had not slipped and fallen from a tree. He fell close to the mine and the skeletons spotted him. In a few seconds, they came out of the mine. Some shooting arrows and others had swords in their hands. Somehow, they managed to pull the frightened player out of danger.

"In a few seconds, they came out of the mine. Some shooting arrows and others had swords in their hands."

The skeletons chased them for a long time. MinerJack and his friends ran so fast that they soon lost sight the skeletons. They stayed there for some time and left only after they were sure that the skeletons had left.

Hasty plans

MinerJack sat under a tree deep in thought. He had faced every possible mob in Minecraft and he knew that some were easy to deal with, like zombies. Others like skeletons and Endermen were a little trickier, but he could still easily defeat them. In fact, he remembered facing a group of skeletons out in the open, one time.

He'd stepped away as far as he could and started shooting arrows as he spun round and round. The trick had worked!

"So why am I having a problem with a bunch of skeletons over there?" MinerJack spoke out aloud.

MinerJack realized that the skeletons were too quick and fierce. They did not give anyone time to think or react. And they all wore armors, and it made it difficult to shoot them easily. The other thing was that the skeletons were not out in the open. It made it difficult to tackle them without coming within their attack range.

There was only one way - One group should bring them out of the mine and another group could hide and attack them with arrows.

MinerJack was excited. That would work! He told this plan to the other players and villagers. But nobody was willing to be in the group that had to bring the skeletons out of the mine. They could get hurt by the skeletons, right?

"Why don't we get them out in sunlight? They'll catch fire!" a villager said.

"It didn't work... we tried. They just don't catch fire," said MinerJack.

"Or why not shoot arrows randomly inside the mine... who knows, it might kill them," said another player.

"I believe somebody tried this. From what I know, more skeletons spawned after that," said MinerJack.

The Wise Priest

There was a long silence.

"There's one thing we haven't done yet," said a villager. "We haven't spoken to Ren, the priest in our village. He's old and very wise!"

The other villagers nodded. MinerJack smiled.

"That's a very good idea. Let's ask him what we can do!" he said.

Together, they went to see Ren. He listened to them and rubbed his hands slowly.

*"He listened to them and rubbed
his hands slowly."*

"I don't think they're ordinary skeletons. Somebody has cast a spell on them. I believe it's the witch who lives in the forest," Ren said slowly.

"So isn't there any way to defeat the skeletons?" MinerJack asked.

"There are many ways to destroy the skeletons if you thought hard enough," said Ren, mysteriously. "But it's not just enough to destroy them. You need to break the spell. That is the only way to free the mine from them. Otherwise, the witch will send another set of skeletons or spider jockeys or whatever she fancies..."

"What do we need to do?" asked a villager.

Preparations

Ren cleared his throat.

"It's not easy to get rid of them without the help of an enchantment. Ordinary splash potions, swords and arrows will not do," said Ren.

"What else will destroy them?" asked MinerJack.

"There's a desert not far from here. Go north and then due east until you find a big cactus. Walk straight on until you reach the desert temple..." he said.

The others listened.

"I believe you'll know how to reach the hidden chamber without blowing up the TNT. Check all the treasure chests. You will find one enchantment book in one of the chests. Bring it to me and I'll help you defeat the skeletons and save the diamond mine," said Ren.

MinerJack stood up.

"We'll do as you say," he said. He looked around. "Who wants to come with me?"

A villager and two players were willing to accompany him on the journey. They set out in the evening and travelled all night. They rested for some time and reached the desert early in the morning.

In the Desert

The moment they spotted the cactus, they heaved a sigh of relief. It was good to know that they'd not lost the way or reached another part of the desert.

Just when MinerJack thought that they'd been lucky to have not come face-to-face with any mob, he saw a witch straight ahead. She was standing with her hands held over her hips. Her nose moved all around her face, making her look scarier!

The witch dug into her robe and pulled out a slowness potion and threw it at them. They all ducked at about the same time, and the potion went past them and smashed on the ground.

The potion of poison was next. This time, they all sprang out in different directions. It fell on the ground and broke.

CLINK!

She pulled out the potion of harming next. She threw it straight at MinerJack, who pulled out his sword.

WHAP!

He struck with all his might and sent it crashing. Now was the time to attack. He dropped his sword, pulled out his bow and sent arrows whizzing. Three arrows struck the witch and she fell on the ground.

Together, they made their way past her and ran as fast as they could.

The Desert Temple

And soon they saw the desert temple!

"And soon they saw the desert temple!"

They entered inside and began to dig quickly. That was one way to reach the hidden chamber without setting off the TNT.

Soon, they emerged into the chamber. MinerJack smiled. They'd chosen the spot for digging perfectly. They'd missed the pressure plate that activated the TNT by many inches!

MinerJack hauled himself up and the others followed. They opened all the treasure chests.

"Here it is!" cried the villager. He showed a big enchantment book in faint velvet cover with a red ribbon around it.

They made the journey back to the village quickly. Ren's eyes shone when he saw the enchantment book.

The miracle potion

Ren read the book carefully and found a page at the very end of the book.

"Ren read the book carefully and found a page at the very end of the book."

"Not all enchantment books have this potion listed. It's found only in this book in this desert temple," Ren said softly.

He took the book and went into his room where he had an enchantment table and all kinds of ingredients.

MinerJack sat outside the room, listening.

THUNK! CLANG! HISSSS!!!

Finally, Ren came out and held a tiny bottle triumphantly.

The liquid inside the bottle was a light purple color.

"The liquid inside the bottle was a light purple color."

"Behold! A magic potion to reverse any spell!" Ren announced.

"Now, who's going to go and throw this bottle into the mine?"

Everybody looked at MinerJack.

"I'll do it," he said quietly.

"Throw it into the mine. When it breaks, it'll release fumes. That will break the spell," said Ren.

"So will I be able to kill the skeletons easily after that?" asked MinerJack.

Ren smiled. "If the potion works the way I think it will, it won't be necessary for you to kill them."

"Good luck!" the players and villagers chorused.

The Great throw

MinerJack felt thrilled. He took the tiny bottle and walked towards the mine. He remembered that there was a bush close to the entrance. He went there and looked at the mine.

RATTLE! RATTLE!

He heard the low rattling noises of the skeletons as they moved around. MinerJack gripped the bottle in his hand.

Maybe they'd realized that there was somebody within their attack radius. Without wasting any more time, he threw the bottle straight into the mine.

BOOM!

The bottle fell straight through the mine opening and exploded.

MinerJack watched as purple smoke filled up the space.

There were a lot of noises inside.

RATTLE! RATTLE!

THUNK! CLINK!

CRASH! WHIZZZZ!

He thought the noises were never going to end. He went towards the mine, with his bow ready.

But suddenly, there was silence.

Mining At last!

When MinerJack peeped inside, he was astonished. All the skeletons were lying on the ground. Arrows and swords were scattered everywhere. They had attacked each other!

"Wow, what a potion," MinerJack thought.

He whistled loudly twice. Players and villagers came from all directions.

He pointed inside and everybody crowded around.

By evening, players and villagers walked freely inside, mining and bringing back heaps of diamonds.

MinerJack went to meet Ren that evening and gifted him the biggest diamond he found in the mine.

Trapped in Minecraft

Ricky - Minecraft Addict

Ricky went by the name Ricky007 in Minecraft. He loved playing Minecraft! You might love playing it all through the evening before you go to bed. But Ricky sometimes woke up in the middle of the night and played the game. Whenever he was in the Minecraft Universe, he forgot that he was in his house.

He went right into that world, played there and stopped playing only when he had achieved whatever he wanted. Then he'd look away from the screen, stop playing and go back to sleep.

The same thing happened when he played Minecraft with his friends at their homes. While others managed to eat popcorn, grab a cold drink or talk about school, Ricky became Ricky007. He ate steak, apples and bread, drank milk and interacted with the villagers, all in Minecraft.

Yes, Ricky was addicted to the game.

A Long Walk

Ricky's friends often teased that one day he'd never find his way back to the real world.

And it really happened!

Ricky was tossing and turning in his bed one night. He opened the curtains in the hope that the cool breeze would help him get back to sleep. He drank a glass of water, but that didn't help either. He knew exactly what he wanted – a dose of Minecraft. He had to play the game, right away.

He jumped out of bed and didn't bother to switch on the light. Soon, he was inside the Minecraft world. He was in a desert and there was a large cactus on one side. The desert seemed to stretch endlessly. Ricky007 was in no mood to tackle mobs, mine diamonds or build fortresses. All he wanted to do was explore.

Just for fun, he decided to simply walk on and on along the desert to see what he could find.

He was fully awake now and he had a lot of time! He walked on and on. He had his sword in hand and his bow slung across the shoulder. He was ready to deal with anything on the way.

The Signpost

The sand dunes seemed to stretch on and on like an ocean!

"The sand dunes seemed to stretch on and on like an ocean!"

After about an hour, Ricky007 saw something in the distance. It was a broad wooden plank and a stick – a signpost.

"What is a signpost doing in the middle of nowhere?" Ricky wondered.

He went closer and read it. Then he frowned and shook his head.

"Am I dreaming?" Ricky007 wondered. He read it again.

"Welcome: Ricky007. This is Advanced Challenge mode. NO EXIT to your world until you accomplish mission. Mission: Get the Emerald Armor."

"Somebody's idea of a joke," Ricky muttered and laughed.

No Way Back Home

Ricky peeled his eyes away from the signpost and decided to take a break. Maybe he was playing too much, every day.

The only problem was he couldn't even see his home.

He looked all around, but everything was from the Minecraft world. Any direction he turned, he could see only sand. His room was nowhere in sight!

Ricky007 was very scared. Surely, something like this could never happen.

Ricky tried to think of his room, but he couldn't. All he could see was sand everywhere. He closed his eyes and opened them again, but it was no use.

He was well and truly caught. He had no choice but to take up the mission.

So how was he going to get the emerald armor, whatever it was, without any clue of any sort? Was this Mission Impossible?

In Quest of Emerald Armor

Ricky007 knew that there was one thing he needed to do – to retrace his steps and go back to the place where he had started.

From there he meant to look around and find the nearest village. He needed to talk to villagers and players and find out about the armor.

It took him a long time to go back all the way, but finally he saw the cactus.

"It took him a long time to go back all the way, but finally he saw the cactus."

Ricky007 rested for a while and walked south.

Luckily, he found a village and he did not see any mobs on the way. It was a good thing because even though Ricky007 was very good at tackling all kinds of mobs, he was feeling nervous and frightened.

Wouldn't it be terrible if you can't return home unless you find an emerald sword?

Ricky007 had to complete the mission – his whole life depended on it and it was no game. He looked around the village, trying to find someone he could talk to.

Finally, he found a villager standing by himself.

"Hello," Ricky007 called out. "I'm supposed to find an emerald armor. Do you have any idea where it is?"

The villager shook his head.

"But if you have something to exchange, I can give you emeralds if you want. Want to trade?" he asked.

"No thanks," said Ricky007 and moved on.

Information at Last

He went talking to one villager after another but nobody knew anything about an emerald armor. Ricky007 knew that an emerald armor was impossible to make. Then where was he ever going to find one?

By evening, Ricky007 felt like crying. Nobody seemed to have a clue. He might never find the armor! He decided that he was doomed to live there forever.

He sat down on a low wall and stared at the ground gloomily. Who was ever going to talk about an emerald armor?

And at the moment, he heard a voice.

"...imagine how great it must be to have an emerald armor! Nobody else can make it..."

Ricky007 looked up, thunderstruck.

It was a player talking to a villager.

He rushed over and grabbed the player's hand and demanded, "Who has it? The emerald armor? I want it..."

"Hey," said the player surprised. "I and my friend met Steve in the forest a few hours back. Steve had this really awesome emerald armor and I wanted it so badly..."

"So do I..." said Ricky007. "Where is this forest?"

He got the directions from the player and set off.

Finding Steve

Ricky007 reached the forest early in the morning.

Hunting for Steve inside the forest was no easy task, but it was better than wandering around hopelessly all over the world, looking for the armor.

He climbed up the tallest tree he could find and looked all around. Not far away, he found a clearing and what appeared to be a small structure.

Ricky007 decided to go there. Steve might be there.

He walked through the forest until he reached the clearing. He looked around. He heard a low rustle in the distance and saw a figure approaching.

It was Steve!

"It was Steve!"

The Fight

And in his hands was the shiny, bright emerald armor. It dazzled and shone like a hundred stars.

"Want it?" Steve asked, grinning. "Too bad... I don't lend it to anyone!"

"I'll fight you for it," said Ricky007, pulling out his sword. He rushed towards Steve. He swung it at Steve with all his might.

CLANG!

Steve had pushed his armor against the sword and turned around. He tried to stab Ricky007 with his sword, but he ducked quickly.

They fought on and on. Steve had a great advantage with the armor. It was the best in the Minecraft world!

In the second that Ricky007 stared longingly at the armor, Steve jumped and pushed the sword towards Ricky007.

Ricky007 fell to the ground, the sword aimed at his throat. He felt tired and closed his eyes.

Mission Accomplished

Ricky007 knew that if he did not get the armor now, he was never going to go home ever again. It was a terrible thought. He knew that he had to act, and act quickly.

He struck with his foot with all his might and aimed a blow on Steve's leg.

THUNK!

It was completely unexpected and a powerful kick.

Steve fell down.

Ricky007 kicked again and sent Steve's sword flying in the air. It fell into the bushes.

He aimed the sword at Steve. "I win!" Ricky007 said. He pulled the emerald armor out of Steve's hands.

The very second, Steve disappeared and a signpost appeared magically.

This was the message:

"Mission Accomplished!"

Ricky rubbed his eyes and turned around. He was back in his room. He slept soundly that night.

Did you think Ricky would be scared to play Minecraft ever after?

The next day, he couldn't wait to play again.

"What is the next mission going to be?" Ricky thought. He was already excited.

Willy's Triumph

Minecraft Craziness

Willy was a good and well behaved boy who was 9 years old. He lived with his parents and two siblings, Jack aged 14 and Sarah aged 11. His brother and sister were attending middle school. They would usually go on their own. They would come back only to stay in their rooms the whole day. Willy was in elementary school and would be joining their school from next term. He was too excited to go to a senior level school now.

"It would be fun and interesting," he thought.

Read Or Play?

Jack and Sarah were always busy. Mom and Dad had bought them an Xbox 360 and they both were also proud owners of iPhones. They spent a great deal of their time playing games, especially Minecraft. Time would pass by quickly when they were playing the game. They wouldn't even notice that. Only later they would realize how much time they had spent playing games.

"Oh gosh! I still have homework to do!" Sarah would say.

"I am feeling sleepy now after playing Minecraft for such a long time," Jack would say.

They would both take a nap or relax, ignoring their studies most of the time. That had created their grades in school to drop significantly. Mom didn't know about this as she trusted all of her children and was always very busy with her own work on the computer.

Willy Wants To Play Too...

It so happened one day that Jack and Sarah were enjoying Minecraft when Willy came along. He looked at each of their gadget's screens from time to time and really got interested in the game. He watched Jack fight the skeletons and Mirrinda build a wall to protect herself from the creepy looking spider. Now he wanted to play too! "Oh please, Oh please let me play Minecraft too!" he pleaded to his brother and sister who were occupied with the game.

"Oh please Jack, let me play with you", he said to Jack.

"No, no, you are too young to play Minecraft," said Jack, " You are too young to encounter such terrible monsters. You will be scared of them."

Willy now ran to Sarah and said, "Oh please Sarah, let me play with you".

"No, no, you are too young to play Minecraft," she said, "You will let the Endermen get you. You are not strong enough to face the dangers in Minecraft."

"But I am old enough. I am strong enough to face all kinds of dangers. Just let me play once and I will show you," Willy shouted.

But Jack and Sarah did not listen at all. They didn't let him the game even once. Willy had no choice but to leave them alone. Then he rushed to his neighbor Alicia who was also playing the same game.

"Oh please Alicia, let me play Minecraft. Just once," he said to her.

But Alicia also ignored him. She said, "No, No, you are too young to play Minecraft. You will drown in the deep waters or get lost in a dungeon."

"But I am old enough. I am strong enough to face all kinds of dangers. Just let me play once and I will show you," he cried.

But nobody was ready to listen to him at all. He felt terribly upset and wondered what to do. Then he had an idea!

Willy's Idea

"Yes, I will ask Mom. She has always stood by me and she will not refuse, I am sure of that," he wondered. He got up and found his mother working on the computer as usual. He told her how much he was longing to play Minecraft but nobody was allowing him to. His mother smiled. She gave him a big hug and said, "Ok, I will let you use my computer to play Minecraft but only if you promise me that you will be a good boy, mind your manners and finish your homework on time." Willy was more than glad and he immediately accepted his mother's offer.

Now it so happened that while Jack and Sarah were not paying much attention towards studies, Willy had become more studious and attentive at school and at home. He would be always very eager to finish his work so he would be free to use his mother's computer. He started playing Minecraft and very soon got the hang of it. He could easily combat the enemies and scare away the ghosts. He found the game adventurous yet fun. "This is a wonderful game," he thought. It was quite addictive and Willy spent a lot of time learning new strategies and tricks to find his way through the dungeons and look for gold bars and diamond swords. A few months went by and Willy was playing better than before.

Minecraft Competition

One morning, at breakfast when the family had gathered at the table, Sarah very proudly announced, "A competition has been ordained on the Minecraft official website. Anybody securing the highest assets in the lowest time limit will win a year's worth of scholarship fee at any school. I am definitely going to participate and I am sure to win.

Nobody, just nobody stands a chance against me."

When hearing this, Jack said, "Oh come on Sarah, there's just no player in the entire world who can beat me at Minecraft! I will be the winner for sure".

Willy heard them and said, "I will also participate and show you that I am just as good." Jack and Mirrinda gave squeals of laughter and Willy stayed quiet.

"Ha! You silly thing, you can't even tie a shoe lace. And you say you will enter this world class competition. Ha ha ha!", Jack cried out.

Willy did not say a word to them. He secretly made up his mind to enter the same competition.

That afternoon after he finished his homework, he visited the site and read all the details. He got himself registered with his real name and set off to practice. One week's time was given during which each participant could log in and play. Each participant could play only once. The scores would be recorded and the person with the best performance would win. Willy spent a great deal of time playing Minecraft and learning new traps and tricks the following days. On the last day, he logged in and played the game and he did very, very well. He was proud of his own performance. Jack and Sarah had also played and so had Alicia. All of their scores were recorded.

At school, aptitude tests had to be taken the following weekend. Willy performed really well as he had already practiced for all the activities and assignments. However Jack and Sarah had a hard time preparing for them. They struggled to fulfill their requirements on time. Mom had a tough time with them and she was very angry!

A few days went by and the result of the competition was to be announced. Jack and Sarah along with Alicia, Mom and Willy, logged in on the site, felling excited. The three of them were far too confident they would win but... but.. what's that? Who's the winner?

On the screen, in large, bold letters was written the name of the world champion of Minecraft. It said:

"Willy Robinson, aged 9, River Primary School is our new World Champion. He has won a year's worth of school scholarship fee and a brand new iPhone."

Jack and Sarah stared at the screen, then gaped at each other, then turned back to Mom who also stared at Willy. Willy was smiling and he shouted loudly, "I told you! See, I told you! I am old enough. I am strong enough to face all kinds of dangers. I have shown you!!"

A Lesson Learned

Jack, Sarah and Alicia felt embarrassed at their previous behavior. They promised that they would never ignore younger siblings and never think low of them. Moreover, they promised to always give top priority to studies.

Now you must be wondering how each of them performed in the exams? Willy passed with flying colors! Whereas the other three kids had average grades and their teachers and Mom were upset with their performances.

A GREEDY MINER

Once upon a time in Minecraft, there was a very greedy miner. He was very, very greedy and selfish. He would always keep everything for himself and would never bother to share it with anyone. One very hot and sunny day, he was busy mining in his cave with his pickaaxe and other tools. He was hungry and thirsty and was about to leave the cave when his axe struck something. He heard something cracking.

CRASH ! CRACK !

"What was that? It sounded like glass," he said, "I will dig further very carefully and find out." Then he dropped his axe and started to dig with smaller lighter tools using his hands as often as he could so as not to break any more glass from whatever was there down below the earth.

THE TREASURE MAP

It took around 30 minutes to dig out a small crystal clear glass bottle that contained a piece of old paper inside it. "Oh how I hope it's a map to some hidden treasure," he said out aloud. He opened up the bottle cap and turned it upside down to make the piece of paper come out. With trembling hands, he opened it up to see that it really was a map leading to some hidden treasure. "Eureka! I have found it! Now I will be rich, richer than anyone else in the whole world of Minecraft," he shouted with joy. He studied the piece of paper and found out that the route was long and tough. A lot of obstacles were to be handled during the way. He was supposed to travel over mountains, through caves, cross many lakes and more. "Should I ask someone to assist me? Oh no… why should I? Its better if I go alone… too many cooks spoil the broth", he wondered, "On top of that, I will have to give half of the wealth to my partner, so why take anyone? I will take all the riches hidden there and build a castle for myself. I won't give anything to anyone… why should I? After all, I will have found it so I am the righteous owner."

"With trembling hands, he opened it up to see that it really was a map leading to some hidden treasure."

He saw two other fellow miners walk inside the same cave that very moment. He hid the note of paper in his pocket. "Hey Johnny, what have you been up to and what was that?" one of them called out. "Oh nothing much, that was the doctor's prescription. I am about to go out and enjoy the sun. Its dark in here," he answered. He did not dare tell anyone about it and went out.

Out in the sun, he searched for a few weapons and tools that would assist him during his journey to the hidden treasure. He picked up a diamond sword, an axe and other useful items that might come in handy during the trip. He walked and walked following the instructions on the map. He was very tired and the sun made him exhausted. At last he reached a village and saw a well. But unfortunately, the well was dry and there was not a single drop of water. He started looking for any villagers when all of a sudden a group of Zombies appeared. They were coming quite quickly. These Zombies had large fireballs in their mouths which they started to shoot towards him.

"Oh my, oh my", said the miner," What should I do?"

Immediately, he shot towards the left and to the right and continuously swapped his position until all the Zombies had gone by.

Kind Horsemen

He felt very tired and weak. He was about to take some rest when all of a sudden he heard a group of men talking. He turned around to see several men on horsebacks.

"He turned around to see several men on horsebacks."

They stopped when they saw the tired, half collapsed miner and one of them said, "May we help you?"

"No, I don't need any help, thanks for asking," replied the miner.

"Are you sure? You don't seem healthy. We are going near the Rocky caves now. Would you like to come with us?" said one of the men.

"Oh no, I don't need any help," replied the miner.

Now the miner continued his trip. He was supposed to reach the Nether Fortress situated in the midst of the Hanama Island. This island was in the middle of the Acid River and was famous for its army of Withers. The miner reached the Rocky caves and was about to enter one of the caves when suddenly hot molten lava poured out from inside.

"Shoot!" he cried out," Where did this come from?"

He quickly reached for a ladder and climbed it high enough for the lava to flow underneath him. He was safe. Finally he reached the cave marked "X" in his map. He went inside and walked all the way through it, attacking and dealing with all the creepers and monsters that came in the way.

"Finally he reached the cave marked "X" in his map."

The Hanama Island

When he was coming out, he saw a huge lake of crystal clear water. The water was so clear that the bottom of the lake was visible and some strange fish and other sea creatures could be seen. The mysterious Hanama Island could be seen in its midst. On top of that the magnificent Nether Fortress was visible.

He reached for a boat and started his way towards the island. He had just left the shore when something strange happened. His boat started bobbing up and down and he lost control over it. He was terrified. Suddenly he saw what was causing the boat to move. Huge bones from skeletons were present in water in such large numbers that they were causing the boat to move abnormally. The miner heaved a sigh of relief and with great difficulty he reached the island.

THE WITHER ARMY

He pulled the boat on the shore and reached the island. He started off towards the fortress when a Wither spotted him. The Wither was a soldier keeping guard and he paged his officer that a foreigner had appeared. On hearing this, the official sent the entire Wither army to deal with him. In a jiffy, Wither soldiers started marching towards him to take him into custody.

He was very scared. He took out his weapons and tools and started to fight but it was totally useless. There were now as many Wither soldiers to be seen as the amount of hair on his head, it was totally impossible to defeat them. The Wither official captured him and took him to the fortress where they tied him up in the corner of a huge hall.

The hall was very dimly lit and he was given no food or water. The miner could see that it was the same hall that was marked on the map. He saw a huge marble statue and knew at once that the treasure was hidden behind. But how could he reach it? How could he fight off all these Withers? The Withers were present all over the fortress now. They had increased the security of the fortress. The poor miner sat there and thought, "Oh how I wish I had asked somebody for help. Oh how I wish now I had not been so selfish. Oh God, please send someone to help me. I promise never to be selfish again." He started crying with pain in his body and didn't know what to do. He fell asleep.

THE ARMY IS DEFEATED!

Suddenly he woke up. "Hey what's all this commotion?" he cried out. "Where are all the Withers?" The hall around him was empty and he could hear a great sound outside. It seemed like a great war had broken out. The sounds continued for an hour and the miner could sense there were multiple players outside who were attacking the Withers. "But who is there?

Will those players help me in any way? What if they decide to take away the treasure and run away with it?" he wondered.

The huge door opened and the miner was surprised. The same horse men he had met some time ago during his journey were all there! They had also found the way to the treasure and had collected together to form a small army to reach the place. "We don't know each other. We belong to different countries. But we are all united through Minecraft! Minecraft bought us all together on this platform and here we are! We thought it was better to get united against the enemies, two is always better than one, you know. By the way, we intend to distribute this wealth to the poor and needy all over the world".

THE TREASURE IS FOUND!

One of the kind horsemen quickly came to help the miner and untied him. The miner was glad to be freed but he felt very guilty about what he did earlier. All the other horsemen went to the marble statue to look for the treasure behind it. They found a huge treasure chest that contained lots of precious items. They opened it up to find valuable ornaments, diamond swords and gold ingots. They all shouted out in joy. As for the greedy miner, he had learned the most valuable lesson, far more precious and important than the riches they had discovered – to always be ready to help the needy and never to be selfish, and to be thankful for whatever you have.

"They found a huge treasure chest that contained lots of precious items."

Zombie Island

In search of diamonds

Trevor, also called TMiner, wanted some diamonds.

He had lost many times to other players and he couldn't tackle the mobs, especially Endermen and Zombie Pigmen. He thought and thought about it and decided that the problem was with the sword. It was an ordinary iron sword. He knew that a diamond sword was the best for fighting.

But he didn't have a single diamond with him! And nothing useful to exchange for diamonds with the villagers.

That left him just one option – mining for diamonds. He'd searched for a whole week and didn't find a single mine anywhere.

His friend took pity on him and told him that there was an island not far off, where there was supposed to be a mine with many diamonds.

"But nobody has explored it yet," his friend said. "Want to wait for me to join you?"

TMiner shook his head. "I'll check it out right away!"

Building a Raft

TMiner might not be good at fighting players or mobs, but he was very good at building things! And he had all the materials he needed for it.

Within an hour, he had built a strong and sturdy raft. He was proud of it. He stood facing the sea and shaded his eyes to see in the distance.

Yes, there was an island. It looked lonely and lifeless.

"Yes, there was an island.
It looked lonely and lifeless."

"TMiner pushed the raft carefully into the water. As it bobbed up and down gently, he leapt in and held on until the raft became steady. He pulled the oar and dipped it into the water and pushed. The raft began to bob up and down first, and then became steady.

He rowed the raft carefully along the water. By sunset, he was very close to the island.

The Island

He noticed that there were trees everywhere and what seemed to be a series of caves in the distance. It was a good sign! There might be diamonds inside those caves waiting to be mined.

As he came closer, he wondered why it was deserted. It was so easy to make a boat or raft and travel over here! He expected more players to be roaming around, mining diamonds and building fortresses.

As the raft touched the shore, TMiner leapt down and tied the raft onto a rock.

He felt uneasy because it was so quiet there. He stood at the shore and looked around again. There wasn't anybody there! TMiner felt a little scared and wished somebody was with him.

But it was too late anyway! He was on the island and he decided to make the best of things!

"I'll get some diamonds and leave at once," TMiner thought.

Looking Around

TMiner slowly walked around the island, peeping into the caves and looked out for mobs. It was a pretty small island, and it took him only a few minutes to walk completely around it.

He decided to go back and check if his raft was safe and go into the caves.

He climbed up the rock and slid down on the wet sand and looked up.

His raft was gone!

"Where is my raft?" TMiner stammered. He was shocked. He didn't understand how a raft could go missing in a place where nobody was there. It could not have drifted away. He had tied it to the rock carefully.

For the first time, TMiner felt a shiver run down his spine. There was somebody in the island and there was no doubt about that!

The First Zombie

TMiner looked around for a few minutes. There was nothing else to do but look around again. He had to find his raft.

"But first, I'll make a fire," said TMiner. He sat huddled close to the fire, staring at the flames.

RUSTLE.... CRIK!

The sound of pebbles and gravel crackling made TMiner look up. Somebody was approaching him.

TMiner stared in surprise when he saw who it was.

A zombie! TMiner grabbed his sword and got up quickly to strike it down.

"A zombie!"

But most surprisingly, instead of hurrying over to attack, the zombie stood still and raised his hand.

TMiner put down his sword.

"Welcome, player," the zombie said slowly.

"Uh?" TMiner looked surprised.

"This is... our island, but you can stay here as our guest as long as you wish!" said the zombie. "But first, come and meet the others!"

More Zombies

"My raft?" TMiner suddenly remembered.

The zombie turned around. "It's safe where it should be. But come along, everybody is waiting!"

TMiner wasn't sure what he was doing, but he went after the zombie.

Soon, the zombie went towards one of the largest caves. It was closed with a smooth flat rock. But the zombie knocked on another rock and all of a sudden, the rock slid open to reveal a long passage.

"Come inside, guest! This is our home," said the zombie.

TMiner stepped in and the rock slid back into place.

TMiner felt a little uneasy but he followed the zombie. They went through the passage and into a wide space. There were hundreds of zombies everywhere and in the center sat one zombie.

"You've come at last!" the zombie said. "We've been looking for a suitable king for this island, since I'm getting old!"

The Chosen One

TMiner felt proud. Did they think he'd make a good king? True it was a small island with only zombies, but it was so thrilling to become a king.

"There's only one thing you need to do…" said the zombie seated in the middle. "Eat a plate of rotting flesh…"

"But it's poisonous!" TMiner said.

"No, we cook it in a special way!" said the zombie. "You rest for a while here… it'll be served to you!"

TMiner was taken to another cave where he lay down and thought.

He decided to go for a walk.

The Wicked Plot

He saw that there were a lot of tunnels in the cave. They were large and spacious. He was about to go past a tunnel when he heard voices.

"That fool believed everything..." one voice said.

"...once he eats the rotting flesh, he'll become a zombie like the other players," said the other voice.

Then they both laughed.

TMiner was horrified. So this was their evil plan and all the zombies here were once players! This was terrible news.

But until he had a plan of action, TMiner knew that he had to pretend to be innocent. He went around looking through all the tunnels in the cave. He found one passage particularly bright and glimmering. When he went inside, he found diamonds strewn all over the place. He grabbed a handful and stuffed it into his pockets. In the next tunnel, he found his raft.

Escape!

When the plate of rotting flesh was brought in, TMiner said that he had to go out for a little while as he wasn't feeling well.

The zombies nodded. They didn't know that TMiner knew everything.

Without wasting a second, he rushed to the tunnel, dragged out his raft and ran out of the cave as fast as he could. He had a few minutes to escape before the zombies came after him.

He huffed and puffed as he dragged the raft over the rocks. He pushed the raft in the water.

He was about to jump in when a zombie came over to him with a sword.

TMiner pulled out his own sword.

WHAM! SLASH!

He struck at the zombie with all his might. With one final blow, he sent the zombie flying to the ground.

"He struck at the zombie with all his might."

CRASH!

He knew that more zombies would arrive there soon.

He jumped onto the raft, pulled out the oar and rowed as quickly as he could. In the distance, he saw a group of zombies watching him from the shore.

TMiner was so glad that he'd managed to escape! He had enough diamonds to make a sword and anything else he wanted. He felt bad for the other players who'd been turned into zombies. He decided that he'd return to the island soon with a spell to transform the zombies into players!

GET YOUR COPY OF PART 2!

Available on Amazon.com
as an eBook, audiobook and in print.

Minecraft Kid's Stories 2:
A Collection of Great Minecraft
Short Stories for Children

25029966R00086

Made in the USA
Middletown, DE
15 October 2015